Momentary Dark

BOOKS BY MARGARET AVISON

Winter Sun (1960)
The Dumbfounding (1966)
sunblue (1978)
Winter Sun/The Dumbfounding: Poems 1940–66 (1982)
No Time (1989)
Selected Poems (1991)
Not Yet But Still (1997)
Concrete and Wild Carrot (2002)
Always Now: The Collected Poems (3 volumes, 2003–2005)
Momentary Dark (2006)

Momentary Dark

MARGARET AVISON

McCLELLAND & STEWART

Copyright © 2006 by Margaret Avison

All rights reserved. The use of any part of this publication reproduced, transmitted in any form or by any means, electronic, mechanical, photocopying, recording, or otherwise, or stored in a retrieval system, without the prior written consent of the publisher – or, in case of photocopying or other reprographic copying, a licence from the Canadian Copyright Licensing Agency – is an infringement of the copyright law.

Library and Archives Canada Cataloguing in Publication

Avison, Margaret, 1918-
Momentary dark / Margaret Avison.

Poems.
ISBN 13: 978-0-7710-0887-0
ISBN 10: 0-7710-0887-2

I. Title.

PS8501.V5M64 2006   C811'.54   C2005-906042-5

We acknowledge the financial support of the Government of Canada through the Book Publishing Industry Development Program and that of the Government of Ontario through the Ontario Media Development Corporation's Ontario Book Initiative. We further acknowledge the support of the Canada Council for the Arts and the Ontario Arts Council for our publishing program.

Text design by Sean Tai
Typeset in Sabon by M&S, Toronto
Printed and bound in Canada

This book is printed on acid-free paper that is 100% recycled, ancient-forest friendly (100% post-consumer recycled).

McClelland & Stewart Ltd.
75 Sherbourne Street
Toronto, Ontario
M5A 2P9
www.mcclelland.com

1 2 3 4 5   10 09 08 07 06

for the Pearl poet

The Gold I gather
Is drawn up
Out of deep Water.

Like a shining Fish
Then it descends
Into deep Water.

   – Rudyard Kipling,
      from "The Runes on Weland's Sword"

Contents

Milton's Daughters: The Prototypes	1
Scarfover	3
Political Ploy Perhaps	4
Not Words. Alone.	5
A-luff	6
In the Earthen Kingdom	7
A Weather Front, Early Spring	9
Harvest	10
Beneficences	12
Lemmings	14
Prayer	15
Exposure	16
High Overhead	18
Rhythm	20
Bereavement and Postlude	21
Finished When Unfinished	23
Reconnaissance	24
Is Intense Sincere?	26
Poetry Is	27
Making	29
Songs	32
"Thy Kingdom Come"?	34
3 a.m. by Snowlight	36

Why Not	38
The Implicit City	39
Diadem	41
Abandon	43
Comment/Comeant	44
This Day	45
Hot Noon	46
Find a High	49
Wanderer	50
Spaces, Verticals	52
Where Is Everybody?	54
Best Foot Forward	55
Window Conversation	57
Prayer of Anticipation	58
Grades of Intensity	59
Seen	60
In September	62
Two to One	64
No Dread	66
Palette	68
A Hearing	69
En Route	71
horror humani	73
Looking Back	75
Exchanges and Changes	77
Never Alone	79
Shelters	80
Acknowledgements	91

Momentary Dark

MILTON'S DAUGHTERS: THE PROTOTYPES

Children of celebrated
fathers, how do you find
your haven? Maybe you
escape to a cousin's or
a married sibling's? If
there are two homes, off and
on separately (the
parents'), would you be governed
by where you have little but private
stress to cope with?

(With her mother away,
Deborah Milton had to be used,
by ear and pen especially,
at her alternate home.
Imagine, in the deeps of night,
the blind man, haplessly resounding with a surge of
line upon line till he could
bear no burdening more, and at
4:30 a.m., the hired
amanuensis ill!)

You heard, and wrote: a process
bypassing mind, or heart,
I'd guess.
Did sister Mary too
have to learn how to pronounce
those many languages
he wanted read aloud?

Children of dust, summons can come at
difficult hours, disrupting
the sleep of nature.
The voice must be
heeded, the incomprehensible
words forming at best
a promise that,
somehow, someday, everything will
come into clarity.

Warm-hearted Samuel
Johnson must have been
exasperated
on your behalf, saying that you
had been schooled only
in alphabets and sounds
of Greek, Arabic, Hebrew,
not in the words, the
meanings that might have
made the long hours a little
less deadly.

Daughters, sleep well
while time runs on.
Rise, docile, dim
of spirit. Someday someone
will bless you for it.

SCARFOVER

Glorious, rigorous, sun-flooded,
snow-iced morning,
scoured by the north wind, marble-hard to today's
human designs,

we do not dare defy you but
still our defiance is
summoned up. We are
human creatures,
resolute. We'll go
our this day's way,
plunge into, become party to
the frieze of this iron and
brilliant, uncompromising
artwork,
its foil.

POLITICAL PLOY PERHAPS

Is
Humpty Dumpty a
was?
His all-apartity
awash
in royal horses?
(as likely to squash
that goggle-eyed face
in the grass as
to reass-
emble a torso from as
many bits as hash)?

Perhaps poor Humpty had
to tumble so we'd see
all the pieces we need
to make democracy.

NOT WORDS. ALONE.

A sky-blue world in the dark of
outerness may find
no echo but emits
squeakings and dots (human).

                        Would that
these might transmute, become a

diapason to the ear of
some vigil-keeper on some
body far away out there but like
enough our earth's body – or to an
unsuspended silence.

Although no transience lingers, may
all the myriad noises of our
everyday doings never,
may they never give us away
out there, tell to a
universe who we are.

                      No
normal sounds can travel on
beyond our little skyspace.
No. Or at least
let's tune these up together
a little, first!

A-LUFF
(*a-luff* OE "on the windward side, heading into the wind")

The sunrise window shrills
with the east wind of
wind-wild March.

The watching listener is
aloof:
a-luff – behind
glass-glare but lolloping
out on the deep

where cresting green
and crystal comber-drops
plunge into sea-moil, for
this blink of time within
a new creation's new

morning. Let ear and eye
and raw-voiced joy
join, jolted into re-
creation's: "Let there be
Day!"

IN THE EARTHEN KINGDOM

As the skies feel their way to
where I sit, the unrhythmic
taps for attention (rain on the smudgy
glass) are like the
whole wide sky wanting to
tell me something. Its
language slowly submerges me in
an unfamiliar
long-ago event:

a daughter, with a
mother who had all the
say as well as a
large family, knew.
She had known what
the woman was
capable of doing. She
was not
out to keep herself safe,
and sane.

She watched while one by one
that woman wrecked her sons'
wholeness, let alone any
hope of independence. Maybe
the daughter and the baby –
always somebody else's
responsibility – had
mattered too little, early on?

If mama later did
remember these two, they'd
somehow escaped her in
escaping her notice.

Off in an alien land
a doyenne and a brave young fellow
sat down awhile together,
snug behind glass,
visited by rain, sensing its storytelling tap-tap-tap
as though, today perhaps,
it might be telling
me, or anyone far away,
one episode from the
skywide saga of the
kings and royal
heirs of an ancient city
open to any now who has an
ear to receive this echo
borne down the centuries.

A WEATHER FRONT, EARLY SPRING

What do I breathe
this darksome day, that is being
squeezed moistly out of the overcast, a
seeping vaporous sludge
into the lungs?

No industry's
foul breath is being
forced on those at the
pedestrian level, but
pressures build. The
car exhaust creeps in
as well. All
builds toward a far
sure, exhilarating
storm. It will blow in

an applegreen evening. How
the limp trees then
will all be plumage-tossers! And
we people will
walk out into
the last skyshine
to breathe, again.

HARVEST

My great-great-grand-
father (on mother's side)
built, behind his new
farmhouse, a
small corn-crib on stilts. He was
homesick perhaps for the
Old Country's rainsoak where
mowers worked against a darkening
light, eyeing the edged-with-
white-ash leaden piling-up
storm clouds.

Was he snoring? No. He
was murmuring:
"Thunderheads they call them in
this country.
In harvest season, here, in the
barley-sweet late summer's heat
they simply leave the stooks
in the stubble to
dry, till harvesters can
fork it all onto
toppling wagonfuls ready for
winnowing, sacking,
marketing, and for the hayloft
and barn."

My great-great-grandfather's
memory was

exact; particulars he
prized. My memory is
faulty now and he is
long in the earth, readying for
the final harvest.

BENEFICENCES

I know of only two
ways into the
person-freeing silences.

One calls for an interval in
solitude. It is
an unemphatic, unremarked
fugitive pang of beauty:
perhaps a glimpse of green
hillside suddenly
sunlit; or
a Percy Grainger melody happily
playing itself unasked within an
absent-minded moment.

The other way is even,
although unbiddable, simpler.
For some occasion the
everyday acquaintances have
gathered, congenial people, none of them
individually central, just
familiar. All are focused
outside ourselves. Some
core validity rings out from one
pronouncement, or the build
of a cathedral of
words or music: it is
absorbed, and, not
predictably,

suddenly generates
that communal oneness, the
rare person-freeing silences.

Other ways there may
be. Hoping so is
what makes living
go on, go on.

LEMMINGS

In cruel office shoes
Five o'clock ladies pound
past, toward their release.
(They're homeward bound.)

Where are the office men?
Spoiling their appetites
with snacks (those on the wagon)?
or having "a quick one"?

When the tide's at full spate
some hasten toward the trains
not free to contemplate
coffees, or wines.

Ladies – a meal contrived
and basic order too –
welcome the men they wived.
"Clean-up's for you!"

PRAYER

In the cold February sun
I sit, silent, with a presence
not known within. Yet, known?

For the cloud, of unknowing
(not of night or day
or time or place),
I yearn as David did for
springs in a dry land.

Let the unknowing
structure what
is known. Let
what "they" think they know
be three ways verified, once by the
human hearer who
proved He could be trusted
in death, in life, always.

Let inner hearing
create listening, so that
the presence not here
(not yet?)
may speak.

EXPOSURE

Every living thing
as a mass or a
morsel, or one who moves with
the speed of light, alike –
each, in His miracle of
particularity,
the Lord knows.

What is left, as though unknown
by the Knower's and
the rebel's mutual
consent, the psalmist calls
chaff in the wind.

Even a pear on a
leafy July bough,
or a begrimed
pear on a downtown fruit stand,
or a pale piece of pear in a
hospital dish proffered
a toothless mouth,
blank now toward
sustenance, and breath:
even such pears also are
known.

But unlike other
living things
being slow, slow, to learn

in this interlude,
life, just being under
the sun, we
vacillate between awe, and
apprehension lest we be known.

The Knower, knowing, waits
our turn.

HIGH OVERHEAD

Late spring: misty mid-
morning sun
flattens mere earth with the
girth of its far but
fatherly presence up there.

There is another sun
for all our sun's
family to respond to too, though
far more remote, to us in a
wide earth-morning rather a
book-fact than even a shivery
minimal awareness.

Is it up to us too to
hold steady, not
"irregardless," but irresistibly
going straight on? Far out there, surely,
the hotly earth-embracing
swerve will happen, will
steady the too-
rambunctious heart.

Galaxies: what a metallic
wind-fierce word!
Great stones are out there, possibly
ore: not ours to mine;
no one's to prospect even; we are

(contemplating such vastnesses) homesick
for springtime's cedar-sharp
freshness here, now, this
misty mid-morning, where
we live and, breathing, are simply glad
on our own little rollicking orb.

RHYTHM

Colour and quietness
embrace the place of
listening, of brilliant
awareness. This
necessitates a widening
rift from the clamours,
the dense
smells and stupidities of us all
out here – the
very core of why anyone
would want to
listen, communicate
quietly. Ever that
rift widens.
But the calm of the
channel water
ruffles, and
in time, boils. And the
need for that
sunbright glade aglow with
fireweed begins to
seethe as well.

Rhythm of living, es-
tablish your ways
under our nonlongsuffering
bewailing, sense of some-
thing lost, always.

BEREAVEMENT AND POSTLUDE
(Remembering Angela Bowering)

O lovely, in a failing light
to find again the never-levelling
valley under sepia airflow
where, in farm-dark, lies all one shore
but for the prick of lights at some small jetty.

How wide the waters here, how
seamless: sinews of the current
swell and relax, perpetuating
the silting detritus of bygones
none can remember now.
On the far shore, see? away over, *there*:
some little village twinkles down to bedtime.

"Far from my valley
a tasselled evening shines around me here,
nowhere a ripple or any curl of foam
to lip the brittle air;
no one to sit here, too, quietly, with
listening heart, aware of the
wide waters silvering my silence."

Grief that had gouged
so long
has deepened to the sorrowful
majesty of
an unknown valley. Families dwell there,
far scattered; weary after chores, their days
one with the relentless riverflow . . .

                    Sweet still, the waters in their amplitude
are powerfully borne,
rippling down to
widen and smooth out like a
morning sheet being spread
on a thin mattress,

moving massively into
the engorging brine, its
voiceful everpresence.

FINISHED WHEN UNFINISHED

On a flat stone, in the
plain light, lies a
torn paper with something written
on it. All the wide shore, the
calm lake, the reeds
listen in the sun, in
silence, as do other flat stones.

Writing to read? for a bird in
transit, or for the
breeze that sometimes stirs when a
motionless midday
passes? No one
is left, writer or some
incurious wanderer now
long gone.
                    Here is only
peacefulness, and several sunny
flat stones.

RECONNAISSANCE

Signs and symptoms
speak out, but when
embossed on persons are
rarely discerned in
preventive time. And

who heeds a warning
posted ahead and out of
sight of a dangerous
stretch of highway?

Earth-dwellers tend to
amble about in spite of
being alerted: "unsafe"
or "stay out
unless you have good reason
to enter here."
It's the wording. "Probably
all a dead issue,"
the tone as flat as the map
of a land that ends in a
knife-edge over nowhere.

Signs and runes
gleam out in the last
tapestried evening sky.
Symptoms, all spent, open on
silence.

Seek out the person who
endures here. Or two or five
perhaps, or a thousand thousand. They
are the heretofore
unknown. Necessity
held them in reserve
as, ultimately, sign and symbol.

IS INTENSE SINCERE?

Neither passion nor
prophecy is
poetry. They come before, or are
premonished. Prophecy has its
force from both, though
one may dominate – a detriment with
a few exceptions!

Prophecy and passion become
poetry after,
after long bearing-with.

Yes, the sixteenth century
poets were light on prophecy.
Singing does that to poets – remembering
that Shakespeare always is the
exception. Desdemona's
presence remains private to herself.
Only to Miranda, calm
and undemanding, came the
sea-wideness, the sure
promise of sungold towers
with Ferdinand, exalting, at her side.

That comes of exile.

Largely out of our reach
the divine passion is
prophetic, yet
unchangingly fulfilled.

POETRY IS

Poetry is always in
unfamiliar territory.

At a ballgame when
the hit most matters
and the crowd is half-standing
already hoarse, then poetry's
eye is astray to a
quiet area to find out
who picks up the bat the runner
flung out of his runway.

Little stuff like that
poetry tucks away in
the little basket of other
scraps. There's the

cradling undergrowth in
the scrub beside a
wild raspberry bush where
a bear lay feet up feeding
but still three rubied berries
glow in the green.
He had had enough.

Then there's the way
a child's watering can
forgotten in the garden
no faucet, but the far

sky has filled. When sun
shines again it has
become a dragonfly's pretend
skating rink.

Scraps. Who carries the basket?
What will the scraps be used for?
Poetry does not care
what things are for but is
willing to listen to
any, if not everyone's,
questions.

It can happen that poetry
basket and all *is*
the unfamiliar territory
that poetry is in.

MAKING

This is not mist. It's myriad
snowflakes, the fine-grained kind. Our roof
breathes them. Their roof is
mothering cloud-mass. Its roof is
sun and air. Their roof
goes black, where space creates
dark context for
lovely blue-green solitary
little earth.

If one who'd lived in heaven
once wanted to
find his own way and walk it, so was
hurled out, to plummet down,
horribly down, in ancient
time
(which was a time of
beginnings, from
where we came in) –
then why would You
make us, foreknowing that the
earthen people would, before
long, have their own notions and
hide out,
hoping against hope they
hadn't been caught?

                        You
who are not time-bound,
committed Yourself to this
odd creating (even though Your
imagination had been riotously
playful, spindling out a
universe, with many
minor and massive whirlings and
vast arenas where they can wheel).
Why, here, a
coddling space around
one little orb, clothing it
with air and seas and continents and
tiny life-forms, magical in
detail, most of them, too,
minutely alive?
                        Such
elegant, such lovely
patterns and impulses, each
unique in every
new-minted morsel!

Yet You
foreknew us who would
muddle, mangle, despoil, degrade – moreover, with
a mind meant to
be like Yours.

How privileged we are! and
how paltry.
            Patiently nonetheless
You have created us

too, and quietly
proceed toward the
ultimately irreversible
mortally perilous
purpose: Your
"delight"!

Just now a glint of
sunlight on glass alerts me.
That massive cloud has all
come underfoot, unsullied white.

SONGS

Inclemency must be right-
angled, upright, sovereign, foolish
under the eyespread of night and day.

The source of song – by the brook Kishon, by
the waters of Megiddo – ancient records
gloat over, appropriating all
the conquered's inclement cruelties.

Today's, tomorrow's blood-stained
jubilation jolts us, remembering
too late.
The alternative fended off is still
icy in our bones.

Why is the source of song when we
gather in the gloaming, or indoors
when winter snarls and hurls
rattling grains of snow against the shutters,
why is a peaceable company nourished on the
songs of railroad strikers, of
shipwrecks, disastrous cyclones, fires
engulfing whole communities

as the strumming storyteller
renders these? (Icelanders
crowded along one edge in the bunkhouse
and rocked with the rhythm, listening.)

Is the clemency
all in the singing narrative?

Odd, that any
quietude can be
menacing. Too many long
(foolishly) for the
right-angled, upright, sovereign voice, the
singing celebrant, one foot up on
the prone subjected first.

"THY KINGDOM COME"?

Whenever we muttered those words, I
dimly saw
a heavy crown, golden, with little
gems all around, descending from
out of the blue above the clouds
and the church roof.
When once it had established royalty the
kingly emblem would
vanish into thin air.

Today (was it the "come" that
did it?) that ponderous visual
failed. Instead, a vibrancy, a
current, an inaudible anthem made
my ears attentive. From
what source? What for?
Is this some distant angel's heralding?

A king is, in a kingdom,
usually remote. It's his
authority that, in a kingdom, matters, and
our liege-salutes, our little
curtsies, or an indecorous
excitement ("How
glossy! How the horses toss their manes!
What dazzles of fireworks to-
night, sky-wide!")

When with the others I
muttered "Thy kingdom come,"
were we praying for
if-it-did?
or, heaven help us, it
did, it *had*, and
we had missed the
moment?

               A kingdom lasts
long enough for everybody's
moments: we
rightly relax about it.
And yet we keep on saying
"come," somehow vaguely
envisioning the "kingdom" that
will.

3 A.M. BY SNOWLIGHT

Skies are worth watching.
Yes, for the weather-wise:
some look
to graphs and charts, calculate, show us
shawled (radar) countryside
from up outside of it.
But they look up
too, noticing like us
the silvery overcast.
(See how the trees are stretched, waiting
in trust, even in thirst.)

Skies are worth watching
for all who are or will be
soloing there.
Bush pilots in the early days,
untamed as gulls asweep,
exulted in air currents, in
those colonnades and towers, were
given utterly
to that light-riven spaciousness.

What might emerge today beyond
the street's overcast stretches when
eyes are down; only wet
cement to mirror a gleam, for day
on day?

See that pedestrian's
face! He's stopped on the
curb at a traffic light:
he looks up past
trucks and cars, past patchy walls
to what there is of sky, and is
rewarded. One
golden shaft
lights up the backdrop, ruffles
the nimbus, all its space a
sudden proscenium
with promise of
action, curtain going up.

Skies are worth watching.

WHY NOT

"Muse is a verb, but she
is a lady sometimes, yes?
Musings are intricate, but why
not a lyric next, if you please?"

"Oh very well – if only
the lady Muse will deign
to move such an ungainly
ponderous pen as mine."

For a brilliant moment the sun appears,
makes everything look unreal,
turns icicles into chandeliers,
finds mirrors in glass and steel.

Merriment dances in the twigs
as the winds race over the skies.
Aflap are coat and trouser legs
of the noon-hour passersby.

The winter pigeons, toeing in,
veer from a two-year-old
who is trotting after to see them run
on their bare pink feet in the cold.

THE IMPLICIT CITY

Down, from beyond the
astronomers' farthest
reaches, coming, purposed,
within the scope of
human time: an
opalescent city shall
make its beautiful descent for
human habitation.

>   We *have* our cities!
>   So far they're, yes, far from
>   bejewelled. Tentative
>   people in corduroy jackets or
>   the many in berets,
>   under coiffures, bare- or
>   bald-headed, and children
>   dashing their hair out of their
>   eyes: all are
>   citizens. We keep to
>   the right. Yet often still
>   smash into each other. We go
>   each about his own
>   business, but
>   step over or around
>   the prone or squatting who
>   surely have to have
>   bustling intervals to
>   stay alive. By choice or chance

they sleep where-
ever and whenever they
can. In winter one or two
do not awaken.

Yet O my city, rich as
fistfuls of raisins, down here
already, are you not,
in spite of the
rancid smell, the milling of
every sprig that has
found its foothold through a
broken sidewalk,
are you not, in
some breathtakingly
scary or brilliant moment
momentarily touched by,
bathed in,
a far-breathed holiness?

The one to
come down from the deeps
beyond the vast out
there, up there, will
now, marking
that moment, all the
more yearningly
stretch expectation here
till, almost,
it snaps.

DIADEM

The weight of your glory in its
incarnate's innocence, with your
holy humility: what a
burden, a royal
crown like that!
                       You
slept here unprotected on the
ground usually, after,
often, daylong
walking, standing, stooping for
the crippled-potential people.
You wanted as they did for
each to be startled, to
find himself up, and
walking! Your
generosity received.
                              To the
awakened eye, although
sea-wrack green and bronze are un-
promising, fresh growth peers visible forth.

You never
need sleep, now, but
you know how the ground
is for those
still on earth, wanting a
place to lie down even
by day, the nights here
being unsafe.

It is, no wonder, hard
for these to grasp
innocence, faithful
lowliness, glory.

ABANDON

The bells are celebrating, where? Why
can we scarcely hear? Bemused:
what day is this? O listen!
Hear it. Jubila*te*.

COMMENT/COMEANT

The clock's tick
    audible as the
    rain-dripping from
    boughs outside the window
    but the window is in
    a high-rise, too far up to
    share a tree's
    daily experience this time of year,
is a natural music
within a little clock.

Listening for what is
within won't work.

Yet there is a "secret place"*
revealed but not
at will
perhaps
in all, around us, in
readiness for the
receiving.

---

*"The secret place of thunder" (Ps. 81: 7b)

THIS DAY

This morning was all
iced sunshine after a
grey and gusty week.

So blue a sky!

A three-year-old
out with a strolling
parent, in the shadow-
tracings of a winter tree, a young
tree and so graceful,
danced into its design
on the dazzling sidewalk.

His father
paused, curbing impatience with
stirrings of memory.

HOT NOON

The labourer
in a constructed wilderness
is sometimes desiccated.

"I'm weightless, rootless. There's not a breath
stirring, to move me. If
only I could have one last
sip of life! Then
let it be night. For good."

She was
human.

"Give me a drink," he said.
Startled, she let him
introduce himself, or rather, she
did it for him, almost too
struck by his notability. And then
she ran off.

(Who'd listen
to her?) But her shouts
caught many. Some
had heard about him and ran
with the others, reckless in that
punishing sun.

Yes, he was there.
And dry, still? "What

use is a well," he shrugged, "when we
still have nothing?
Here we be though
for good."

In the cool of the evening, in twos and threes
they left, he with his friends.
She watched them fade from view,
sighed, headed her own
way, all but alone. Tomorrow,
or ever, would this day
have to be
remembered? As are
those surprises that
linger, faintly strange and
bright like yesterday's stars
and planets?

Yes, he was there. They encircled him,
awed, curious, eager to
have something to tell about
later. She watched. Sighing she
went her own way then. Tomorrow
the day would have to be
absorbed, alone. It was as
unsurprising, now,
as watching the last light
fade and stars and planets
shine out, far out
for good.

What makes a human being co-
alesce with the other just in
finding something to
belie, forever, her
usual sultry past,
perhaps?

How does the sequel go
after the story we've
heard? Fidelity
tomorrow? or a naturally
unsupported, solitary,
gradually less and less
defensive life? with
reverence now for
anyone human,
even herself.

FIND A HIGH

            place and see
how the skyscape keeps ever
re-forming.
But from high places how to
know the blue of
the first scilla, the crunch of
snow under the heel.
                  The one
pigeon who flew down with the flock when a
seed-scattering woman on a bench opened her
sack – he in the air
forgets, but now
he is surprised afresh
to find that down on the pavement he
is one-legged, must half-
sprawl, half-fly to
shoulder into that scrum.

May he soon after
focus on flapping his
way high into the
sun to the
construction crane's lift-arm, idled at noon.
The whole flock line up there, perhaps
hoping to ride when it begins
to swing again.

WANDERER

The will of God
has been known, but
so gradually, and
in terms so usual
usually, that the person at the wheel
humming along, preoccupied, had
somehow strayed. He faces
a dead end. Summons the force
of his own will: he
thinks; backing into a lane
he turns, finds the right fork
this time, and goes on pleased that his
judgment redirecting him in time
is confirmed as
reliable.

More than reliability was
at issue though. He didn't know he
was under scrutiny?
being let stray, to work it out?

He spins along. No one
he happily realizes is aware
of where he is or when to expect him back.
The freedom of the road as he
discovers at the
dead end
calls for a clearer

sense of direction, closer attention.

That will turn out to be preoccupation; another opportunity.

SPACES, VERTICALS

That house we long ago
built in the B.C. bracken, braced by
fragrant cedar-boughs and small
branches from underfoot,
made us a happy playhouse though at
times shaky; the woven
roof shook down crumbs, letting
fine little feet sometimes drop onto
the nape of the neck.

Standing under the zenith
moved men naturally to
turn it all upside down. No
plumb line needed, they
anchored their teepees from
the ground around, outside.

Wonderful world, your
mountains mass up, high above
sea level, to a
non-geometric balance. Here
to live, we humans usually
measure, contrive, labour, establishing our
space under heaven.

High-rises seem to
soar straight up – or

the old ones do. Now they're making them
zigzag, or jumbleblocky.
(For a safe start, where and how
soon did they hang the little plumb?)

WHERE IS EVERYBODY?
(a dream)

Where is the typical town I knew
with the dark little store
by the stone clock-tower?
Had there been some hullabaloo?
Why did it seem
before I came
they had all run on,
gone home? Alone,
my gliding shadow
was all I saw.

Up from the unseen
park they come,
musicians in golden
outfits. Oh I
was happy to be
there to cheer as they
solemnly play-
ing went by,

but what if they are the enemy!

No wonder everyone else is hidden
but one unknowing and unbidden
here without motive, without reason
overwrought – because caught – in treason?
Worst of all if the residents heard
and the enemy proffered *me* some award!

BEST FOOT FORWARD

The young students, before
a challenge, or an exam,
are soothed to say, "One hundred years
from now what will it matter?"
They gamble, toward a sunny stretch
still out beyond the near
horizon
of dread.

The old ones, on the slippery
slope, their hundred years
having as good as come –
and gone – still stare
beyond this present
time, for steadying.
Downstream the undergrowth
will crowd into the brambly
banks. No trail. And the hiss
of rapids up ahead.
This time they trek
alone, without a kayak?
It seems so.

The roads, the criss-cross
tomorrows,
lead on those hundred years
and more, travelled or
empty under the round
sky. Whatever

your age it's no use dreading
the world that lies ahead,
or wilderness or water
or chimneyed prospects and a
bustling harbour.

WINDOW CONVERSATION
"Brightness falls from the air"

The clouds, the morning
sun are such that
one lettuce-bright tree-tip
over the roofs, like me,
is singled out. We are
sun-gilded.

You smile away
out there.

You are I am
inexpert about timing.
How this instant was
hit upon is
beyond us. We in
passing can
only receive
this befalling, a
blissed one.

PRAYER OF ANTICIPATION

Jesus, interpreter – more,
configurer of all
that has deepened
odd moments for me from
the outset, you are as if
strolling through the
morning, saying those
fierce, or disarming, words
within the word.

If you approach through
a clutter, nothing need
hinder you, who gave
the deaf hearing, and not
waiting always to be
besought, for the
initiative is yours, is the
essential.

It is my best good
to let you speak your
remembered, translated,
printed, painfully
accessible word.

Jesus, disclose
your journeying for
this day's avenues.

GRADES OF INTENSITY

In the sombre twilight
a crimson crescent lurks
behind the jagged skyline,
immense, through the day's murk.

One witness from afar
stares west, dully yearning:
who assembles fuel for
such a burning?

An intruder finds a grate
in the chill empty room.
Fire would feel so good!
But neighbours may be home.

Coming too near
the light: that's the story
of the luminous martyrs'
final blaze of glory.

Oh, that the awesome far
could come – safely – near!
the Unknowable, known as there
and here, welcomed, in fire.

SEEN

Pitiless light, dry
air, the snowless
winter day
exposes everything, withers
even high clouds, those
cirrus ones; they
race before the bitter wind.

How other is
the light who
sees all, but is for so
long, so long, compassionate!

But in the night uncompromising light's
clarity befalls
the sleepless who
lie rigid, resolutely
suffering it,

      under how many
city roofs, behind
apartment walls, in dank
half-basement rooms? A
slumbering city is
blind to the half-smiling
peace old Noah (and all
outdoors, all winter)
clench on, a
promise.

One day, tea towels will
blow on the line
along a
summer evening lane – hushing the
homegoing rush along
the Danforth – north a bit, then
steadily east, behind those
rosy-brick
Greek walk-up
apartment blocks.

There will again
be amber evening light.

IN SEPTEMBER

Little one, still at
home where (in our
case) you trustingly
assume your value to us, even
when we've made your
face flush with tears
in defence of plain
justice. In
time, you see that our
reading of the case had its
own fairness.

What have you gathered around you
against the predictables of
the schoolyard?

Will you encounter there
bullies? fall in with
bad companions who, at the Children's
Library story-time, are part of
the spell, the story's
tension, and relief?

The well-behaved person you were
intent on being
fallen away, you are
an adventurer, all eyes, now
landed on terra nova.

The ones we warned you
against are those in the
group with all the energy
and zip – and these have proved
wondrously accepting.

Yes, little one. You have to be
ready to get along anywhere.
But be on your guard! We cannot help
following, from alas
our widening distance.

TWO TO ONE

It was some torment, those long years when
the "spiritual
man" moved like a
wraith, outside
the "natural man," the one
dogging the other down the
worldways. Sometimes by night
one of them would extort a
"Who am I?" One
alone
knew, one alone.

Instructed that Jesus came, on earth, as
natural man but that
slowly other natural men
sensed in his talk, his eyes, his
instant aside when an
empty hand or cup
reached out, also that he
tangled with the invasive
obstreperous ones, leaving them limp and
livid, often – the natural men sensed that
nature was somehow new here, speaking,
seeing others, responsive, as though
every occasion were
important, but not to the point.

How long one here, one there, pushes
against improbabilities! Have not

dreams become lore
with every tribe and people?
Why not delight in this
equivalent for us, our tribal
particular?

The rift widens between the
man and wraith. He
reconciles himself to
loss, to one – i.e. only
alas the other.

NO DREAD

The trees lift up their crowns into,
in domes and cone and fretwork, up
into this late September sun
unstirring. They are yielded to
the glow of now, before
stripped starkness, jagged,
like a forgotten hat stand, like
an old umbrella's spokes
after its last gust, left
abandoned. They are
ready to let it all
go now.

These are each innocent
of awareness: that the
intricacy or bold
assertion of their structures
will, by the time the snow flies and
until it decorates
and is swept clean again,
be lashed, lashed by
boisterous gales; that
encapsuling ice will
shelter the shoots, uncruelly
crack the young stronger
branches. But all that, that
misty horizon of
time has to open on,
this late September sun

falling in pluming loveliness
whispers perhaps.

Let them this day
lift up their beneficent leafiness,
this unbewildering beautiful
September morning.

PALETTE

Yellow and blue-green young
cottony leaves, in
cloud-shadow and sun, are
four hues over the
wintry rack of branch and tip –
a still becoming form – that summer
trees will enfold fully.

Such blueness in a windy tumbled
sky, and yet so still!
Mist on the lake water is
gashed by an afternoon swimmer;
healing (tiny orblets
of air, resolving welter)
comes even as the
crunch of homebound footsteps
dies away, the towel-draped
swimmer dashing home again
after his icy plunge.

"Laugh before breakfast – tears
by bedtime"? A sudden shower
fans out from camel-coloured clouds.

The little new-drenched leaves
glow in the momentary dark,
dancing.

A HEARING

The magnitude of
mercy amazes, when, as
Will, Your servant, marvelled
we deserve whipping.*

Men craft their clutter, keep
adjusting, shifting tolerances to
to keep their rage well under
the surface tension.

What moves a man to
dredge up post-diluvian
dread of a sovereign's ruling,
incisive, just, barely
bearable?   Such
moments made
men of the Old Testament
fall prostrate. They
spoke of wing-rush, stood
silent, at stretch, before their
hearing.

These we attend still,
bewildered sometimes,
instructed, in
instances, sure of the

**Hamlet* II.2.501

eternal will to
mercy toward
them; not
only for them!

EN ROUTE

Situation: a summer fisherman
had packed away his gear
toward homegoing, but rocked
in the quiet inlet water,
hearing it, hearing
the breezes sift across
Georgian Bay's massive
shore of rock, hearing
the lightsome heartbeat of peace.

The breeze was stiffening.
He hauled aboard
the roped anchor, clumsily
poled away the cliff of shore,
readied both oars, and set out.
In the broad bay the only
rocks to steer clear of
were near that one large island.

The dip and slap had become
bumps out there
on open water . . .

Then what? *Then* what?

The future lay
ahead of him, as of us.
Rising winds can be threatening
here too, for any who

left it too late to
remember to
head homeward. People are
potential crises, scattered everywhere:
on islands, isolated, bobbing about
in small craft far too far
from rescue, at home and
safe, but far too
long waiting. All
travellers sometimes feeling
they wait too long
for homegoing.

horror humani

Is it a stretch of
the imagination to
declare that
somewhere, in one
Sudanese house, a
poet was
smiling to himself over a
book by somebody else when
the distant racket outside
erupted into
crashing, and he and
his papers and book and
house were
abruptly obliterated?

Flanders' fields were
oddly within fast
post's reach of
quiet places across the
Channel where were
people who
were still opening poetry books, readers of
news too, but like some
English soldiers in those
days, anchored against
noises, deep in the
seabed of
remembered quietness.

That difficult, safe place
was to
be broached by
"The War to End All Wars,"
opening a
chasm still unbridgeable. Yes,
decades later new
elegant prose and verse would be
written, and read, but the
private reader relishing his
book somewhere in
his window chair is
this very moment – O why? –
kaputt. The air-raid
"achieved its purpose."

LOOKING BACK

1. Stocky, sturdy, the sun-
   seasoned old man
   craned his neck at the spectator's
   hole in the boards
   on yet another construction site.
   He had not budged when I
   glanced back.

2. "After a full day's work
   home for more coping: he is
   so ill, and failing;
   then it would vex us both
   if the livestock weren't
   seen to. My, what you can
   do when it's called for!"

3. Expecting a baby, the woman
   figures, with her friend,
   how to adapt the apartment
   to a family of four.
   Her little boy, who's been playing
   under the window, suddenly
   shouts, "I know
   BABY!" his body
   eerily remembering. He lies
   on the carpet, half-
   lifts his head.
   Vaguely waving his arms

he pumps with his legs. Then runs
to his mother, and
nuzzles as though
for a final time.

EXCHANGES AND CHANGES

Sufferer of cities, hear me for
green pastures are
everywhere despoiled. Cement and paving
seal off the hope of
loam for more than our
sons' and daughters' lifetimes. Here
is what we have
meantime to learn: to
be, in cities. Here
too are choices, given
the will, and minimal earnings.

                         "Change,
please," chants the street-corner fellow.
Doesn't he know the
verb is transitive? "Change
my lot with a quarter
of your huge holdings! Change
my role, make me a
giver who keeps back
only the minimal means for a
simple life. I'd like
to look employable again, in time to
work again."
                    And then change everything
with not a single despoiler's energies
agglomerating, ever
again. And then
                change everything

one last time – hear me – to
those almost unimaginable
green pastures.

NEVER ALONE

Those sage and cinnamon family
festivals are now
recollected through a
haze of grave-
side standing, standing
amid fine snow and pendulous
gnarled aged none-
theless flourishing trees
deep-bosomed – like
comforting cousins at a
mourners' wake, that other
family festival.

SHELTERS
(for Mary)

In this city, on a day
this dark, why
do the trees gather? why do they
thrive here, as if they were
those ravine trees nearest
the runoff?
                   If it were
full dark in here,
looking up, the starry
night would still
sparkle, through foliage or,
in winter,
branchiness. Care has been
given: some green
or snowy paths among
the trees. A sky-calm fragrance
breathes everywhere.

A city rush-hour route
buzzes and whines just under
this embankment. Once a tire squealing, but
no thump and sprinkling of
broken glass in one of those
horribly silent moments.
They're quiet about it all
down there; or celebratious with
bright tail-lights mornings, and

early evenings as well, after
the equinox.

Away across the valley
houses are heaped, and apartments; these
are glorified briefly every
sunset at the right season.
                    Lives over there
are only partly
private, and at this distance some
show one upper window
lit. Occasional cars are
nosing into their driveways.
Safe for awhile.

Those points of light?
A daughter doing homework with her
bedroom radio playing? The car perhaps,
one home from work but he
forgot an errand. Fortunately it's
not far.

    When it is this dark
    under the roof of heaven
    (daytime or late p.m. or early
    a.m. alike) people
    whether under a thatch or
    rafters or dark-brick gables –
    all go to extremes.
    It is the times.

Nowhere is as inside as a
ship's steerage class.
At least planes keep the lights on
unless
all lights, for all, forever,
all at once go out.

Houses of Parliament – are they three?
two of them inside the
biggest building? Surely not
like Russian dolls?
If it's really like that, the
smallest building *is*
the House.

Houses for visits at
Christmas; meeting of trains
and planes, one or two
little ones making strange, too many
cooks in the kitchen, company
arriving, met without topcoat in
the driveway. Then neighbours and more
friends at the doorbell. "Take off
your boots inside here." The kettle
whistles: somebody's signal
to begin boiling something?
Christmas is what you
breathe
in such a house.

∽

The big old
houses, like that, in older Toronto, are
rooming houses today. Social
workers "place clients" in the
available spaces. These days
there are no room-to-let signs up any
more. There is no room though
it's night and the homeless
woman is with child.

The condos honeycomb up
too far above the
trees and humpy houses. They
are lofty.
The swarms emerge on street level
mingling in and out for
food, and drink if pay will
cover that as well as
daily bread.

"Why did we have to
move? This is a
stifling city. This house is
too narrow. Can we go
back – once winter is over?"

    "Up those stairs
    is a room for you girls. You'll have
    your bed, a table, and
    chairs to do your homework and
    a bureau with its own mirror."

"See, the window is tiny but the
world outside is farther
down, and wide, with bigger and
smaller houses. There's one
with its own sidewalk."

However people round the globe
build, to have secrets or
to feel warm breezes, exposed but
seldom sweltering, others
have burrows but
above-ground, stone, or brick.

Canadian winter nights call up
defences. A transient
devises from newspapers a somewhat
layered sleeping bag. Let him tuck in
under a bridge or on that
grating over the
City Hall garage.

Each of us fixes on our
own way and place.

The small boy sat on the
front steps. He eyed
the stranger hesitating, clutching a
bit of paper, glancing
down, then up. "Is this
no. 56?"
"This is my house," he said,
despatching her.

Some people spill their
families around and
in among any
others outdoors. Are they
one brood? or some
cousins too, perhaps? Maybe the
uncles and aunts will come
later. How do they all
bed down inside?

         "Is it
okay if I bring him home for
supper?"
      That's neighbourly but
Oh my, what may ensue?
"Of course, if *his* mother says so too."

Wayfarers may know
such hospitality perhaps; may
linger, learning virtuosity in
the communal rhythm of
clatter and calm, and ritual places
for food, for sleep, for
somehow beginning to be "old
Joe," or "Uncle Joe" for good.

~

Solid structures sometimes
crumble here and there: someone
takes an apartment, another
goes north for work. One daughter
marries! The yard and doorway fill with

frills, one day. The next
somebody sweeps confetti off the walk.
"Our days on earth are but a shadow."*

Sisters: when the out-there
seemed against one of us, we
defied them all, from the same side.
Three instances proved it. They are
distinct. And now
forever private, mine. No proof against
a different, habitual, norm.
Members of one family, strangely, are
socially isolated from
each other. Friends are a
part of the unmutuality.
The side they're on together no third friend
however friendly, could
enter. Not till years
later.

A spinney of old women, thin-
branched valley of old men – all
find the sunlight dim;
suffering from weather, still they
stoutly find the watery afternoon
passable, even "good."
Sometimes, storm-stayed
indoors, or when there's
ice underfoot leaving no option,
some gather, fan the embers

---

*I Chron. 29:15b

in company. So, on the
stilts old legs become,
they find their way to today's
communal place under a sheltering roof.
A few are embittered but resigned.
Most are reliving, as
best they can now, their
former joviality.

~

One in an urn under a
stone marker is the first
here with this surname.
Wait. It's my parents' stone. It's lonelier
here than even first grief was. This, ashes
among progenitors', has to do
only with jars of clay, buried, perhaps
soluble. Do those metallic urns
people keep on their mantels
outlive the come-and-go
belonging the initial
householder meant: as com-
memoration, or to ward off
fear of senile forgetting or of
reckless disregard in
an unimaginable future?

Sometimes the "loved one" is
laid under stone or bronze.
In Egypt the embalmed
were set in chambered
mummy cases; no one had

had foresight enough to
dread that one might
one day be prised open, put
on display in an
alien museum for hushed classes
to tiptoe past, looking.

When it is dark although
the cemetery is in
our blindly self-obliterating
city, the trees
gather, encircle
benches and grassy places.
In here, looking up, the starry
night is barely
visible; yet its scent of *far*
breathes gently.

A throughway, yes, buzzes and
whines beyond this quiet place; over
its far embankment houses
are heaped, lives only
partly private, though at this distance vision
touches on just one
upper-storey window; a slow car pulls
into its driveway. Safe for the night.

Acknowledgements

The following poems first appeared in: *The Windsor Review*: "Looking Back"; *Arc*: "Poetry Is" and "Prayer of Anticipation"; *RealPoetik* (a U.S. website): "Political Ploy Perhaps," "Prayer," and "Scarfover"; *Stolen Island Review*: "Milton's Daughters"; *The New Quarterly*: "Find a High," "Finished When Unfinished."

The careful editing of Stan Dragland made some passages clearer and some spots easier to follow. His practised skill is an ornament to his perceptive reading of manuscripts. I am grateful.

No poem would exist without the primary sensitive reader who sees its strength but can be candid about its blurry places and dogged until revisions make it come into focus. Joan Eichner is that reader, for me. My fingers being by now unreliable on a keyboard, Joan both deciphers my cryptic handwriting and prepares successive typescripts until together we reach the manuscript stage. I need to acknowledge with thankfulness her keeping at it on my behalf throughout all stages of a finished work.